FIRE FLIGHT
A Wildfire Escape

by Cedar Pruitt

illustrated by Chiara Fedele

CAPSTONE EDITIONS
a capstone imprint

Published by Capstone Editions, an imprint of Capstone
1710 Roe Crest Drive, North Mankato, Minnesota 56003
capstonepub.com

Library of Congress Cataloging-in-Publication Data
is available on the Library of Congress website.
ISBN: 9781684468867 (hardcover)
ISBN: 9781684468881 (ebook PDF)

Summary: Flames consume a forest, and an owl seeks refuge.
Helicopter wings chop, and water drops to drench the branches
below. Spare, lyrical language takes readers inside the journey of
a screech owl that fled the flames to ride along with a firefighting
helicopter during the 2020 California Creek wildfire.

Consultant Credits
Thank you to Dan Alpiner, the real-life helicopter pilot in this story,
for his assistance in the development of this book—and for
his brave work fighting wildfires.

Image credit: Dan Alpiner, page 30 (A Note from the Author)

Designed by Nathan Gassman

Printed and bound in China. PO 5593

For my forest explorers,
Pearl and Axel — CP

Deep in a California forest grew
a fire,
crunching dry branches, bark, and heartwood.

Flames loomed,
smoke bloomed,
and orange ribbons wove into . . .

. . . owl territory.

One owl,
a little owl,
had nowhere to go.

Air became ash.
Branches turned to dust.
Feathers quivered in the heat.

There was nowhere to go,
but the owl couldn't stay.

With a swift beat of wings,
the owl burst from deep, deep in the trees,
soaring high above its burning home.

With nowhere to go,
it saw a fellow flyer.

Instead of *beat, beat, beat* . . .

it made a *chop, chop, chop.*

It was the *chop, chop, chop*
  of a firefighting helicopter.

  In a gush,
   in a thunder,
    came the *drip,*
         drip,
            drop
      of water drenching flames.

Water soaked ground
where firefighters
dug trenches
to stop fire's path,
cleared brush to remove fire's fuel.

The little owl flew,
higher and higher until it soared . . .

right through the helicopter's open window!

The pilot gasped.

Would the owl attack?

Scratch with talons?

Bite with beak?

No.

Feet gripped the seat,

owl wings paused their beat,

and the only sound was

chop,

chop,

chop.

With feathers that look like the bark of a tree, the screech owl camouflages easily.

But not here.

Big owl eyes turned to stare.
The pilot took
one
amazing
picture.

CLICK!

Would the owl stay?
Or glide away?

The pilot had to fight the fire
scorching the trees below,
but the owl had nowhere to go.

Back for more water,
chop, chop, chop
another *drip,*

drip,

drop.

A *gush,*
a *hush,*
and the owl hung on.

Would it stay?
Or fly away?
Big owl eyes didn't say.

The pilot flew.
The owl held tight.
One more water flight.

Resting wings,
  watching flames,
    hush,
      hush,
      hush
      in water's gush.

  Orange became gray,
 as flames died away.
Making a place for an owl to go.

Then back outside,
with wings stretched wide,
the feathered flyer took a beautiful glide

all the way down
through smoky wet air
to the branches, bark, heartwood, and home
of an owl.

A Note from the Author

On September 4, 2020, the Creek Fire began to burn in California. The fire grew fast, jumping quickly among dry trees and burning down buildings. It went on to scorch 379,895 acres (1,537 square kilometers), largely in the area of the Sierra National Forest.

For more than three months, firefighters worked hard to put out the flames. On the ground, they dug trenches, cleared dry brush, and sprayed water from hoses. In the air, they poured flame retardant and water from planes and helicopters.

Dan Alpiner, a helicopter pilot for Sky Aviation, was one of those firefighters. On October 12, he was dropping water on the fire when a Western Screech-Owl flew through an open window in his helicopter. It landed on the back of the empty co-pilot seat. Alpiner snapped a picture.

The Western Screech-Owl that landed inside Alpiner's firefighting helicopter.

"It's odd to have an owl enter an aircraft," Sky Aviation wrote when sharing the photo on social media. "It's an unexplainable and magical miracle for it to stay with you for several water drops, then leave just as it arrived—safe and unannounced."

When I first read about this story in the newspaper, I was cozy and warm next to my fireplace on a cold New Year's Day, with my husband and children nearby. Reading about a little owl forced from its home made me imagine what it would be like to have to flee my own home—and picture the moment when the owl took a long look at the pilot. Two flyers, dealing with one fire.

I've learned that while fires can be a natural part of a forest life cycle, they are getting bigger and harder to stop. (When the Creek Fire was finally declared contained on December 24, it was the fifth largest wildfire in California history.) Climate change, brought on by increased pollutants in the air, has contributed to extreme drought—and dry forests—in the western United States. Those dry forests burn easily, which can hurt the habitats of humans, plants, and animals . . . including the home of one little owl.

What Can We Do?

We must all work together to take steps, both big and small, to make a safer environment for all of Earth's inhabitants. Here are some actions we can take:

- Walk, bike, or take the bus instead of taking a car.

- Turn off lights and computers when not in use.

- Use only the water we need and no more.

- Find ways to use renewable energy sources like hydropower, wind, and solar.

- Recycle and compost everything we can.

- Learn about climate change, and share information with friends and family.

- Always make sure to fully extinguish outdoor fires.

About the Author

author photo by Burt Granofsky

Cedar Pruitt lives in owl territory just outside of Boston, Massachusetts, where she is a champion for green space. Her home is with her husband, children, and a crew of animals that cluck, sing, and hiss. It's a hoot! When not writing, Cedar teaches people how to connect with one another across their differences. *Fire Flight: A Wildfire Escape* is her first published picture book. Visit her at www.CedarPruitt.com.

About the Illustrator

illustrator photo by Chiara Fedele

Chiara Fedele was born in Milan, Italy, and earned a degree in illustration from La Scuola del Fumetto. Since then, her illustrations have been published in many countries around the world. Chiara loves bright colors and contrast, and her art style uses a combination of mixed traditional media and digital. She has won multiple awards, including a 2018 silver medal for the Sydney Taylor Book Award. Chiara currently lives in Tromello, a little village near Milan, with her family and pets.